STUDY GUIDE

TRUST ISSUES

TRUST ISSUES

JUSTIN GRAHAM

AVAIL

CONTENTS

JUSTIN GRAHAM

TRUST ISSUES

ANSWERING THE **ONE QUESTION**
THAT **CHANGES EVERYTHING**

INTRODUCTION

MAYBE YOU DON'T TRUST
GOD BECAUSE, IN REALITY,
YOU CAN'T BE TRUSTED.

READING TIME

AS YOU READ INTRODUCTION OF *TRUST ISSUES*, REVIEW, REFLECT ON, AND RESPOND TO THE TEXT BY ANSWERING THE FOLLOWING QUESTIONS.

REVIEW, REFLECT, AND RESPOND

What story or statement in the introduction impacted you the hardest—and why?

_____

_____

_____

_____

Sometimes we deflect blame onto others to avoid facing the truth about ourselves. Where in your life have you pointed fingers instead of looking inward?

_____

_____

_____

_____

_____

What's one relationship or responsibility in your life that may have suffered because of your own compromise, inconsistency, or lack of trustworthiness?

_____

_____

_____

_____

_____

> **"SEARCH ME, GOD, AND KNOW MY
> HEART; TEST ME AND KNOW MY
> ANXIOUS THOUGHTS. SEE IF THERE
> IS ANY OFFENSIVE WAY IN ME, AND
> LEAD ME IN THE WAY EVERLASTING."**
> —PSALM 139:23–24 (NIV)

Consider the scripture above and answer the following questions:

If you were to genuinely invite God to "search" you today, what do
you fear He might uncover?

_____

_____

_____

_____

_____

_____

_____

What "anxious thoughts" or hidden motives might be standing in
the way of you becoming a trustworthy person?

_____

_____

_____

_____

_____

_____

_____

What would it look like to not just read this book—but to let it lead you into lasting transformation?

_____

_____

_____

_____

_____

_____

_____

_____

Are you open to the possibility that your struggle to trust God or others is rooted in something unresolved within you?

_____

_____

_____

_____

_____

_____

In what area of your life have you sensed God prompting you to rebuild trust—either with Him, with yourself, or with someone else?

_____

_____

_____

_____

_____

_____

_____

Consider this statement: "Trust is not only a gift that you give; it is a gift someone gains." In what areas of your life have you expected trust without truly earning it?

_____

_____

_____

_____

_____

_____

_____

How has broken trust—whether yours or someone else's—shaped your view of God? What false narratives might you need to unlearn?

_____

_____

_____

_____

_____

_____

_____

The phrase "Can God trust you?" is simple but weighty. What would it mean for your life if you took that question seriously every day?

_____

_____

_____

_____

_____

_____

_____

_____

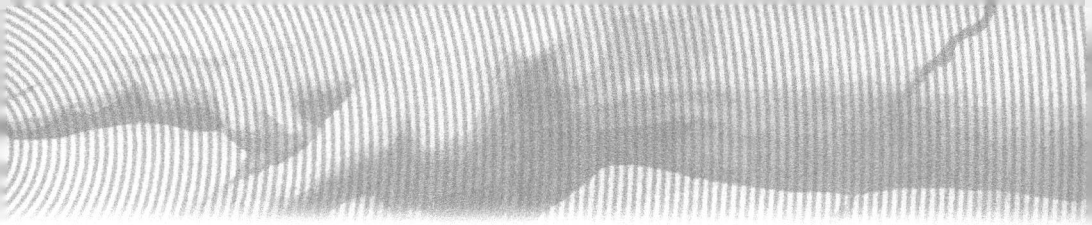

In what ways has a lack of trust eroded your influence at home, in ministry, or in leadership—and how might rebuilding it change the trajectory?

_____

_____

_____

_____

_____

_____

This introduction invites you to deal with your trust issues honestly. What would change if you made that your personal mission throughout this entire journey?

_____

_____

_____

_____

_____

_____

_____

CAN I TRUST YOU?

TRUST IS NEVER JUST GIVEN.
TRUST IS ALWAYS EARNED!

READING TIME

AS YOU READ CHAPTER 1: "CAN I TRUST YOU?" IN
TRUST ISSUES, REVIEW, REFLECT ON, AND RESPOND TO THE
TEXT BY ANSWERING THE FOLLOWING QUESTIONS.

REVIEW, REFLECT, AND RESPOND

If God were to ask you directly, "Can I trust you?"—what would
your honest response be, and why?

_____

_____

_____

_____

_____

In what areas of your leadership or personal life do you find yourself
struggling with trust—either giving it or earning it? Be specific.

_____

_____

_____

_____

_____

When you examine your own heart, what squeaky hinges do you
recognize? What are the trust issues that, if left unaddressed, risk
disrupting relationships with those closest to you?

_____

_____

_____

_____

_____

> "IF THERE WERE PROPHETS AMONG YOU,
> I, THE LORD, WOULD REVEAL MYSELF
> IN VISIONS. I WOULD SPEAK TO THEM IN
> DREAMS. BUT NOT WITH MY SERVANT
> MOSES. OF ALL MY HOUSE, HE IS THE ONE
> I TRUST. I SPEAK TO HIM FACE TO FACE,
> CLEARLY, AND NOT IN RIDDLES! HE SEES
> THE LORD AS HE IS. SO WHY WERE YOU NOT
> AFRAID TO CRITICIZE MY SERVANT MOSES?"
> —NUMBERS 12:6–8 (NLT)

Consider the scripture above and answer the following questions:

Why do you think Moses stood out to God as trustworthy, despite his inexperience and limited leadership skills?

_____

_____

_____

_____

_____

How do you typically respond when others speak against you unjustly, especially those close to you like Aaron and Miriam were to Moses? How do you think that has impacted God's ability to trust you?

_____

_____

_____

_____

_____

When God invites you into a deeper level of responsibility, do you find yourself eager to respond or quick to retreat? What does your reaction reveal about your level of trustworthiness?

_____

_____

_____

_____

_____

_____

Have you ever mistaken a spiritual calling or affirmation for an accomplishment rather than a test of character? How has that shaped your leadership

_____

_____

_____

_____

_____

_____

How often do you surrender your thoughts, responses, and decisions to God in the quiet moments?

_____

_____

_____

_____

_____

_____

Is there a place in your life—whether in your marriage, team, or business—where you know you need to reestablish trust? What is stopping you?

_____

_____

_____

_____

_____

_____

_____

What does it look like for you to live a life that gives God "no trust issues" with you?

_____

_____

_____

_____

_____

_____

_____

_____

Reflect on your digital habits and communication. Can you be trusted when no one is watching?

_____

_____

_____

_____

_____

_____

_____

_____

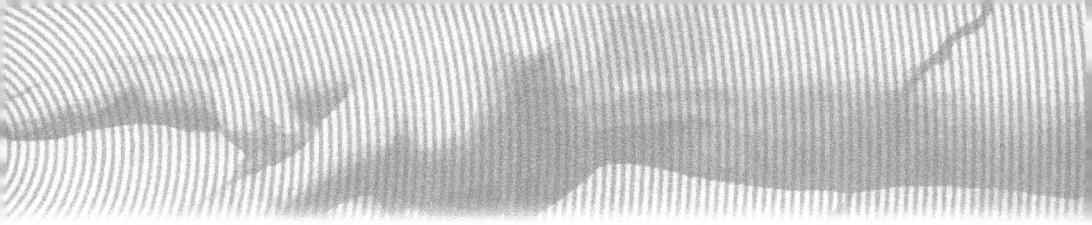

Who around you—spouse, team, children—needs to see your trustworthiness in action, not just in words? How will you demonstrate that this week?

_____

_____

_____

_____

_____

_____

_____

What one area of your life feels "squeaky" right now—the hinge that keeps disrupting the peace of others? What will it take to fix it?

_____

_____

_____

_____

_____

_____

_____

'TIS SO SWEET

WHEN GOD MAKES A PROMISE, HE ALWAYS TAKES CARE OF EVERYONE INVOLVED.

READING TIME

AS YOU READ CHAPTER 2: "'TIS SO SWEET" IN
TRUST ISSUES, REVIEW, REFLECT ON, AND RESPOND TO THE
TEXT BY ANSWERING THE FOLLOWING QUESTIONS.

REVIEW, REFLECT, AND RESPOND

What is one moment in your life where God clearly proved
His trustworthiness to you? How has that moment shaped your
faith since?

_____

_____

_____

_____

_____

When was the last time you tried to "fix it yourself" instead of
falling into God's arms? What was the outcome?

_____

_____

_____

_____

_____

Think back to a moment when fear overwhelmed you. How did you
respond, and what might you do differently if it happened today?

_____

_____

_____

_____

_____

> ## "COMMIT EVERYTHING YOU DO TO THE LORD. TRUST HIM, AND HE WILL HELP YOU."
> —PSALM 37:5 (NLT)

Consider the scripture above and answer the following questions:

What does it practically look like to "commit everything you do to the Lord" in your current season of life?

_____

_____

_____

_____

_____

_____

_____

What fears or doubts tend to hold you back from fully trusting God's involvement in your plans?

_____

_____

_____

_____

_____

_____

_____

_____

What "anchor song" or scripture helps you cling to God in turbulent times?

_____

_____

_____

_____

_____

_____

_____

_____

If someone examined your financial habits, would they say you trust God as your Provider?

_____

_____

_____

_____

_____

_____

_____

_____

When you reflect on past valleys, how has your trust in God grown—or shrunk—through them?

_____

_____

_____

_____

_____

_____

In what ways has your upbringing in church (or lack thereof) shaped how you currently approach trusting God?

_____

_____

_____

_____

_____

_____

_____

_____

Have you ever mistaken God's delays for His denial? How might your perspective change if you saw those delays as divine setups?

_____

_____

_____

_____

_____

_____

_____

"When you work, God rests. When you rest, God works."
What's one area of your life where you need to stop striving and start trusting?

_____

_____

_____

_____

_____

_____

_____

_____

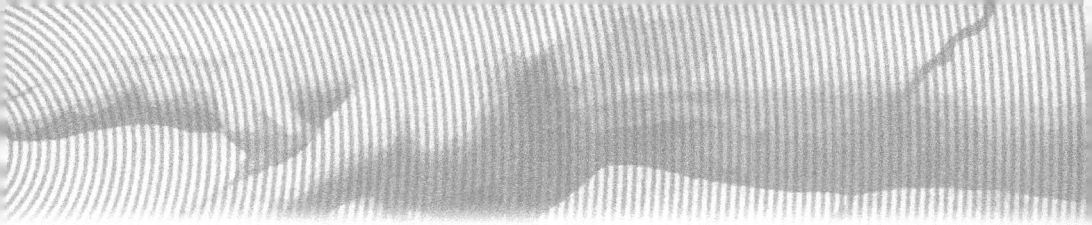

Do your decisions reflect a deep trust in God, or are they mostly driven by logic and self-preservation? Provide an example, and explain what you learned from that experience.

_____

_____

_____

_____

_____

_____

_____

Is there an area of your life where you're still waiting to experience God? What might He be trying to develop in you during the wait?

_____

_____

_____

_____

_____

_____

_____

I DON'T TRUST GOD

HUMANS DO WHAT HUMANS HAVE ALWAYS DONE BEST: MESS THINGS UP AND MAKE MISTAKES.

READING TIME

AS YOU READ CHAPTER 3: "I DON'T TRUST GOD" IN
TRUST ISSUES, REVIEW, REFLECT ON, AND RESPOND TO THE
TEXT BY ANSWERING THE FOLLOWING QUESTIONS.

REVIEW, REFLECT, AND RESPOND

Have you ever been tempted to walk away from God because of something painful that happened to you? What kept you from giving up—or what brought you back?

_____

_____

_____

_____

_____

Describe a time when a closed door led you to the right one.

_____

_____

_____

_____

_____

What's one area of your life where you still wrestle with whether God can be trusted? What past pain or betrayal might be influencing that struggle?

_____

_____

_____

_____

_____

> ## "ARE YOU STILL MAINTAINING YOUR INTEGRITY? CURSE GOD AND DIE!"
> ### —JOB 2:9 (NIV)

Consider the scripture above and answer the following questions:

What voices do you need to quiet in this season so that you can keep your trust firmly anchored in God?

_____

_____

_____

_____

_____

_____

_____

_____

Why do you think Job's wife responded the way she did—and how can you guard against becoming someone who spreads doubt rather than faith?

_____

_____

_____

_____

_____

_____

_____

_____

When trusted leaders fall or fail, how does it affect your faith? How do you separate your trust in God from your trust in people?

_____

_____

_____

_____

_____

_____

_____

Can you think of a moment when you chose to respond to pain with trust instead of bitterness? What did God do in that situation?

_____

_____

_____

_____

_____

_____

_____

"That wasn't God" is a reminder that human failure isn't divine betrayal. What situation in your life do you need to stop blaming God for?

_____

_____

_____

_____

_____

_____

_____

_____

What does it look like in your context to shift from asking "why" to asking "what"? What questions do you sense God inviting you to ask Him today?

_____

_____

_____

_____

_____

_____

_____

_____

_____

If others followed your example of trusting God through hardship, what would they learn?

_____

_____

_____

_____

_____

_____

_____

_____

_____

_____

Who in your life needs to hear that "God didn't do that to you"? How can you be a voice of healing and restoration to them?

_____

_____

_____

_____

_____

_____

_____

_____

_____

What's your next move toward trusting God—not with your words, but with your actions?

_____

_____

_____

_____

_____

_____

_____

_____

_____

_____

_____

HOLD FAST

YOUR CONNECTIONS WILL
DETERMINE YOUR DESTINY.

READING TIME

AS YOU READ CHAPTER 4: "HOLD FAST" IN *TRUST ISSUES*, REVIEW, REFLECT ON, AND RESPOND TO THE TEXT BY ANSWERING THE FOLLOWING QUESTIONS.

REVIEW, REFLECT, AND RESPOND

In moments of deep grief or disappointment, who has "held the rope" for you when your trust in God wavered? How did that support impact your healing?

_____

_____

_____

_____

_____

What stood out to you about Matt Cahoon's story? In what ways did it challenge your understanding of pain, faith, and redemption?

_____

_____

_____

_____

_____

When it talks about "borrowing the faith" of others, what does that mean in your current season? Who around you is offering faith for you to lean on—or who are you offering it to?

_____

_____

_____

_____

> "TWO ARE BETTER THAN ONE, BECAUSE THEY HAVE A GOOD RETURN FOR THEIR LABOR: IF EITHER OF THEM FALLS DOWN, ONE CAN HELP THE OTHER UP. BUT PITY ANYONE WHO FALLS AND HAS NO ONE TO HELP THEM UP. ALSO, IF TWO LIE DOWN TOGETHER, THEY WILL KEEP WARM. BUT HOW CAN ONE KEEP WARM ALONE? THOUGH ONE MAY BE OVERPOWERED, TWO CAN DEFEND THEMSELVES. A CORD OF THREE STRANDS IS NOT QUICKLY BROKEN."
> —ECCLESIASTES 4:9–12 (NIV)

Consider the scripture above and answer the following questions:

What "cords" in your life are helping you remain unbroken—and which ones may be fraying and need attention?

_____

_____

_____

_____

_____

_____

Who in your life is helping you up when you are spiritually or emotionally down? What has their support taught you about God's love?

_____

_____

_____

_____

_____

Are you more comfortable "helping others up" or letting someone help you? Why?

_____

_____

_____

_____

_____

_____

"There are no shortcuts to trust." What long path are you currently walking that God might be using to deepen your trust?

_____

_____

_____

_____

In what ways are you intentionally building relationships with people who will carry you to Jesus when you can't carry yourself?

_____

_____

_____

_____

_____

What is your "hold fast" reminder in this season—something that keeps you grounded and pressing forward through temporary pain?

_____

_____

_____

_____

_____

_____

Reflect on the statement, "I can do anything for a little while." What challenge in your life right now requires that kind of perseverance?

_____

_____

_____

_____

_____

_____

How has shifting your focus from an earthly perspective to a heavenly one changed your outlook—or how could it?

_____

_____

_____

_____

_____

_____

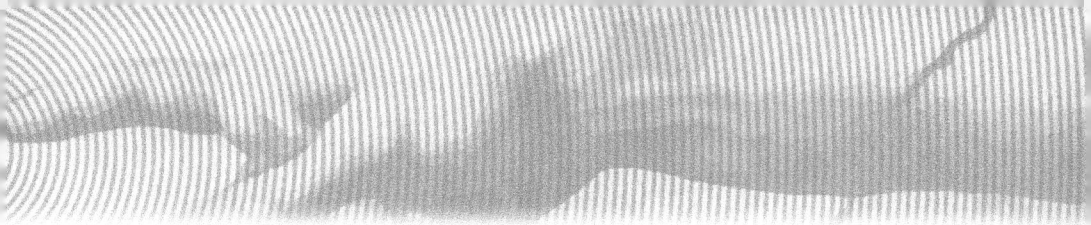

What temporary struggle are you facing right now that could be preparing you for something eternal?

_____

_____

_____

_____

_____

_____

When everything in life feels overwhelming, how do you personally remind yourself to trust God and not let go?

_____

_____

_____

_____

_____

Identify three "why" questions you've asked in difficult seasons (e.g., "Why did this happen to me?"), and reframe each one into a "what" question that will help you take a step forward in faith and trust.

_____

_____

_____

_____

_____

_____

_____

DON'T TAKE THE BAIT

WITH ANY AND EVERY TEMPTATION, PAY ATTENTION TO WHO'S HOLDING THE FISHING ROD!

READING TIME

AS YOU READ CHAPTER 5: "DON'T TAKE THE BAIT" IN
TRUST ISSUES, REVIEW, REFLECT ON, AND RESPOND TO THE
TEXT BY ANSWERING THE FOLLOWING QUESTIONS.

REVIEW, REFLECT, AND RESPOND

What "bait" have you been most tempted by in your life or leadership? How has it affected your relationship with God?

_____

_____

_____

_____

_____

What is a moment in your past where you took the bait—and what consequences followed?

_____

_____

_____

_____

_____

What kinds of excuses are you using to justify behaviors or patterns you know are creating distance between you and God?

_____

_____

_____

_____

_____

> "SO, IF YOU THINK YOU ARE STANDING
> FIRM, BE CAREFUL THAT YOU DON'T
> FALL! NO TEMPTATION HAS OVERTAKEN
> YOU EXCEPT WHAT IS COMMON TO
> MANKIND. AND GOD IS FAITHFUL; HE
> WILL NOT LET YOU BE TEMPTED BEYOND
> WHAT YOU CAN BEAR. BUT WHEN YOU
> ARE TEMPTED, HE WILL ALSO PROVIDE A
> WAY OUT SO THAT YOU CAN ENDURE IT."
> —1 CORINTHIANS 10:12–13 (NIV)

Consider the scripture above and answer the following questions:

When was the last time you were tempted, and instead of taking
the bait, you looked for the way out that God had already provided?
Did you get out—or take the bait? What was the outcome?

_____

_____

_____

_____

_____

Where in your life are you standing a little too confidently—
without the humility and caution that Paul urges in this passage?

_____

_____

_____

_____

_____

Hell doesn't know your weaknesses until you reveal them. In what ways have you unintentionally advertised your vulnerabilities through your choices?

_____

_____

_____

_____

_____

_____

_____

What "good" things in your life have become bait because they've distracted you from your spiritual priorities?

_____

_____

_____

_____

_____

_____

_____

What specific situation in your life is currently luring you toward compromise? What might that "bait" cost you if you bite?

_____

_____

_____

_____

_____

_____

Satan is not a roaring lion—he only pretends to be one. What false power or fear have you given too much authority in your life?

_____

_____

_____

_____

_____

_____

_____

Think back to the "golden calf" story. What modern-day idols are being formed in your life while you're impatiently waiting on God?

_____

_____

_____

_____

_____

_____

_____

When have you felt the Holy Spirit nudging you away from bait and back toward trust? Did you listen—or resist?

_____

_____

_____

_____

_____

_____

_____

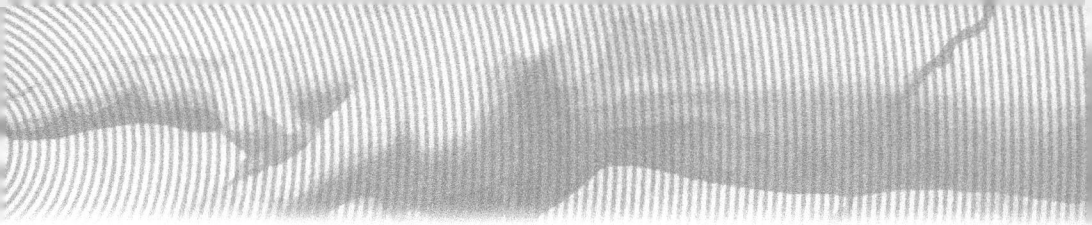

Who in your life models what it looks like to live with integrity and resist the enemy's bait? What can you learn from them?

_____

_____

_____

_____

_____

_____

Write a personal declaration of your commitment to take ownership of the most destructive behavior in your life right now. As you do, thoughtfully acknowledge and incorporate the truth of 1 Corinthians 10:12-13 in a way that aligns with your specific situation.

_____

_____

_____

_____

_____

_____

_____

_____

SHAME ON YOU

FAILURE IS AN EVENT, BUT IT IS NEVER A PERSON.

READING TIME

As you read Chapter 6: "Shame On You" in
Trust Issues, review, reflect on, and respond to the
text by answering the following questions.

REVIEW, REFLECT, AND RESPOND

What are some words or labels that shame has used to define you in your past? How have those labels shaped your trust in God and in yourself?

_____

_____

_____

_____

_____

What are some of your personal "memory triggers," and how do they affect your walk with God?

_____

_____

_____

_____

_____

What do you believe is the difference between guilt and shame? How does one pull you toward God while the other pushes you away?

_____

_____

_____

_____

_____

> **"BUT IF WE CONFESS OUR
> SINS TO HIM, HE IS FAITHFUL
> AND JUST TO FORGIVE US
> OUR SINS AND TO CLEANSE US
> FROM ALL WICKEDNESS."**
> —1 JOHN 1:9 (NLT)

Consider the scripture above and answer the following questions:

What sins do you need to confess to God today? How can you do that without minimizing or excusing them?

_____

_____

_____

_____

_____

_____

_____

How does this verse give you courage to move forward, even when shame tells you to stay stuck?

_____

_____

_____

_____

_____

_____

_____

What is a past failure that you've allowed to define your identity—
and what would it look like to surrender that to grace?

_____

_____

_____

_____

_____

_____

_____

Have you ever disqualified yourself from being used by God
because of shame? What does this chapter teach you about how
God sees you?

_____

_____

_____

_____

_____

_____

_____

When shame whispers, "You're a hypocrite," how will you respond
based on the truth of God's Word?

_____

_____

_____

_____

_____

_____

_____

_____

How do you talk to yourself when you mess up—like a condemned sinner or a redeemed child of God? Provide an example of each.

_____

_____

_____

_____

_____

_____

_____

_____

What "robe, ring, and sandals" moments has God given you to remind you that you're still His and still welcome home?

_____

_____

_____

_____

_____

_____

_____

_____

What "charcoal moment" do you need Jesus to redeem in your life?

_____

_____

_____

_____

_____

_____

_____

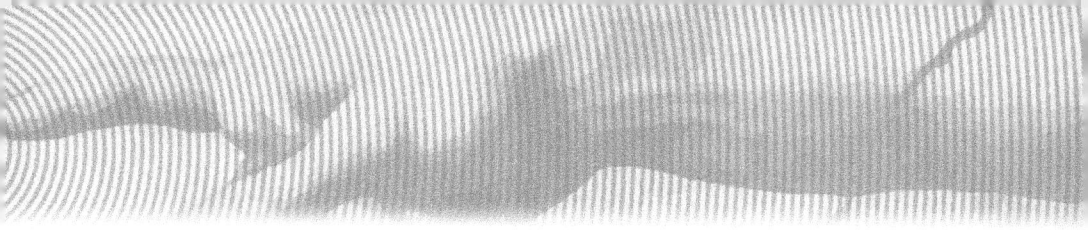

In what ways could letting go of shame remove the barriers that hinder both your trust in God and His trust in you?

_____

_____

_____

_____

_____

_____

_____

What's one physical place, object, or experience you can reclaim and use as a reminder of God's grace rather than your failure?

_____

_____

_____

_____

_____

_____

_____

NOTHING ELSE MATTERS

YOUR PUBLIC PERCEPTION
IS DIRECTLY CONNECTED TO
YOUR PRIVATE PRACTICES.

READING TIME

As you read Chapter 7: "Nothing Else Matters" in
Trust Issues, review, reflect on, and respond to the
text by answering the following questions.

REVIEW, REFLECT, AND RESPOND

Have you ever faced a "Walmart at 2 a.m." moment—where your
integrity was tested in a seemingly small but pivotal way? How did
you respond?

_____

_____

_____

_____

Consider this statement: "Trust takes time to establish and can be
undone in a single moment." What's a decision you've made that
either built or broke trust in a single moment?

_____

_____

_____

_____

When have you, like Moses, let frustration or pressure lead to
disobedience? How did that impact your relationship with God
or others?

_____

_____

_____

_____

> "IF ANYONE CAUSES ONE OF THESE
> LITTLE ONES—THOSE WHO BELIEVE
> IN ME—TO STUMBLE, IT WOULD
> BE BETTER FOR THEM TO HAVE A
> LARGE MILLSTONE HUNG AROUND
> THEIR NECK AND TO BE DROWNED
> IN THE DEPTHS OF THE SEA."
> —MATTHEW 18:6 (NIV)

Consider the scripture above and answer the following questions:

Who in your life looks up to you spiritually, relationally, or professionally? How might your decisions be affecting their faith or trust?

_____

_____

_____

_____

_____

_____

_____

_____

_____

What does this verse stir in you about the responsibility of leadership, parenthood, marriage, or influence?

_____

_____

_____

_____

_____

_____

_____

_____

_____

"If who you are in public doesn't match who you are in private, then who you are in public is fake." In what area of your life do you need to close that integrity gap?

_____

_____

_____

_____

_____

_____

_____

_____

What connections (people or environments) in your life strengthen your integrity—and which ones weaken it?

_____

_____

_____

_____

_____

_____

_____

_____

_____

The story of David and Bathsheba is a cautionary tale about isolation and lack of accountability. Who in your life has permission to call you out when you're slipping?

_____

_____

_____

_____

_____

_____

_____

"Integrity equals zero compromise." Where have you justified small compromises that may be eroding your integrity over time?

_____

_____

_____

_____

_____

_____

_____

Think of a time when someone's lack of integrity caused you to lose trust in them. How might others feel if the same were true of you?

_____

_____

_____

_____

_____

_____

_____

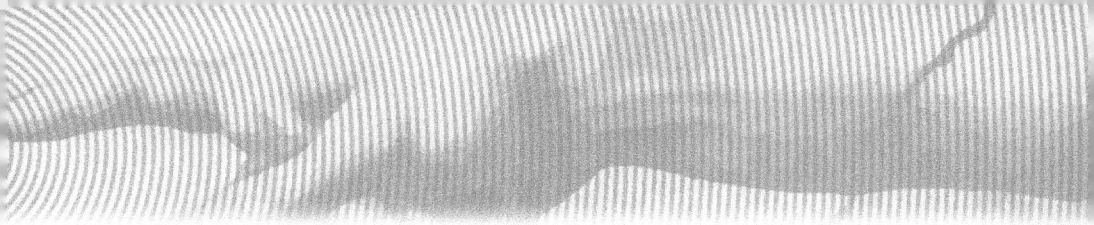

When it comes to your influence in your home, workplace, or church—what do you think God sees? What do you think people see?

_____

_____

_____

_____

_____

_____

_____

What internal shifts need to happen for your heart to be aligned with God's call to live with integrity and trust?

_____

_____

_____

_____

_____

_____

_____

STOP CIRCLING THE MOUNTAIN

SOME PURCHASES ARE NOT WORTH THE PRICE YOU PAID!

READING TIME

AS YOU READ CHAPTER 8: "STOP CIRCLING THE MOUNTAIN" IN *TRUST ISSUES*, REVIEW, REFLECT ON, AND RESPOND TO THE TEXT BY ANSWERING THE FOLLOWING QUESTIONS.

REVIEW, REFLECT, AND RESPOND

What "mountain" have you been circling in your life—talking about but never climbing? What is stopping you from taking the first step?

_____

_____

_____

_____

_____

"Confession and repentance give you access to God's grace and forgiveness. Faithfulness and integrity grant you access to God's blessings and trust." How have you experienced the difference between being forgiven and being trusted?

_____

_____

_____

_____

_____

In what area of your life are you asking God for breakthrough, while still avoiding the hard climb of discipline and integrity?

_____

_____

_____

_____

> **"I DISCIPLINE MY BODY LIKE AN ATHLETE, TRAINING IT TO DO WHAT IT SHOULD. OTHERWISE, I FEAR THAT AFTER PREACHING TO OTHERS I MYSELF MIGHT BE DISQUALIFIED."**
> —1 CORINTHIANS 9:27 (NLT)

Consider the scripture above and answer the following questions:

What spiritual disciplines do you need to strengthen in order to live a life of trustworthiness?

_____

_____

_____

_____

_____

_____

_____

What would it look like for you to live with the kind of intentionality and self-control Paul describes here?

_____

_____

_____

_____

_____

_____

_____

_____

What does "ascending" look like in this season of your life? Where is God calling you higher?

_____

_____

_____

_____

_____

_____

_____

_____

What will you need to release, sacrifice, or walk away from to answer God's call to ascend?

_____

_____

_____

_____

_____

_____

_____

_____

What specific sin or compromise do you need to "divorce" in order to stop circling the same mountain over and over again?

_____

_____

_____

_____

_____

_____

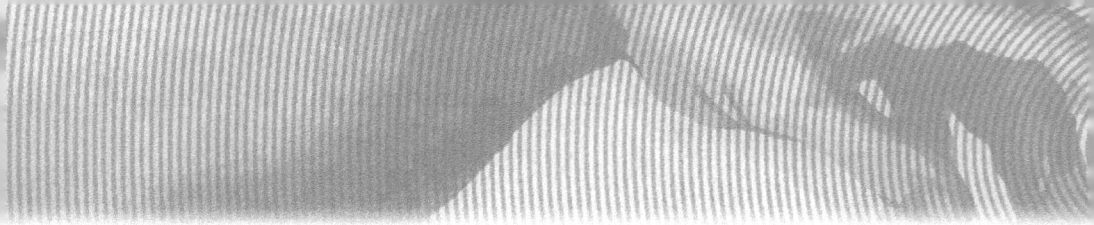

David said, "I will not sacrifice to the Lord my God burnt offerings that cost me nothing." What has your pursuit of integrity cost you so far—and what more might it cost?

_____

_____

_____

_____

_____

_____

_____

Have you been trying to offer God sacrifices that cost you nothing? What would a costly sacrifice look like for you now?

_____

_____

_____

_____

_____

_____

_____

When you look at your life today, are you more motivated by reward or transformation? What needs to shift?

_____

_____

_____

_____

_____

_____

_____

_____

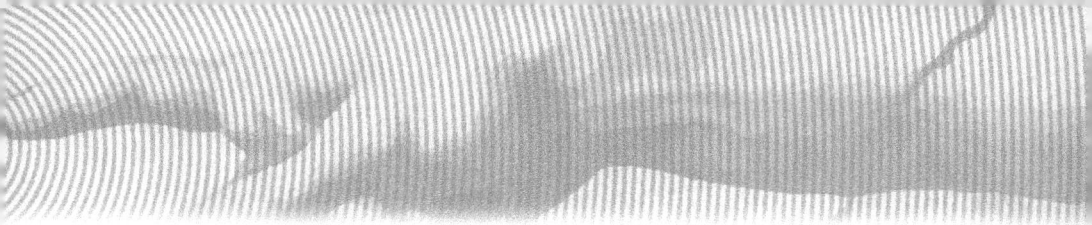

What daily practices, habits, or relationships are helping—or
hindering—your climb? What can you do to remove or minimize
those hindrances?

_____

_____

_____

_____

_____

_____

_____

How are you preparing spiritually, emotionally, and practically for
the next level of purpose God wants to entrust to you?

_____

_____

_____

_____

_____

_____

_____

GOD TRUSTS SERVANT LEADERS

NEVER ASK SOMEONE TO DO SOMETHING THAT YOU'RE NOT WILLING TO DO YOURSELF.

READING TIME

AS YOU READ CHAPTER 9: "GOD TRUSTS SERVANT LEADERS" IN *TRUST ISSUES*, REVIEW, REFLECT ON, AND RESPOND TO THE TEXT BY ANSWERING THE FOLLOWING QUESTIONS.

REVIEW, REFLECT, AND RESPOND

Can you think of a time when you led by example and it deepened someone's trust in you? What made that moment impactful?

_____

_____

_____

_____

_____

Moses wasn't called a great leader—he was called trustworthy. How would others describe your leadership right now?

_____

_____

_____

_____

_____

What does it look like for you to serve in "low places" so God can trust you with "high places"?

_____

_____

_____

_____

_____

> "BUT AMONG YOU IT WILL BE
> DIFFERENT. WHOEVER WANTS TO BE
> A LEADER AMONG YOU MUST BE YOUR
> SERVANT, AND WHOEVER WANTS TO
> BE FIRST AMONG YOU MUST BECOME
> YOUR SLAVE. FOR EVEN THE SON
> OF MAN CAME NOT TO BE SERVED
> BUT TO SERVE OTHERS AND TO GIVE
> HIS LIFE AS A RANSOM FOR MANY."
> —MATTHEW 20:26–28 (NLT)

Consider the scripture above and answer the following questions:

How does Jesus's willingness to serve impact the way you view leadership in your home, ministry, or workplace?

_____

_____

_____

_____

_____

_____

_____

What mindset or ego barrier keeps you from embracing the lowest seat at the table?

_____

_____

_____

_____

_____

_____

_____

_____

Who is someone in your life right now that you need to lead with
more humility and compassion?

_____

_____

_____

_____

_____

_____

_____

_____

_____

How do you respond when others disappoint or betray you—like
Judas did to Jesus? What does that reveal about your capacity
for grace?

_____

_____

_____

_____

_____

_____

_____

_____

_____

Reflect on this statement: You'll never know how to be great until you learn how to serve." What's one area where you can start serving more intentionally?

_____

_____

_____

_____

_____

What area of your leadership needs to be surrendered to God so He can trust you with more?

_____

_____

_____

_____

_____

_____

Who in your circle of influence needs to see your faith in action, not just hear it in words?

_____

_____

_____

_____

_____

_____

_____

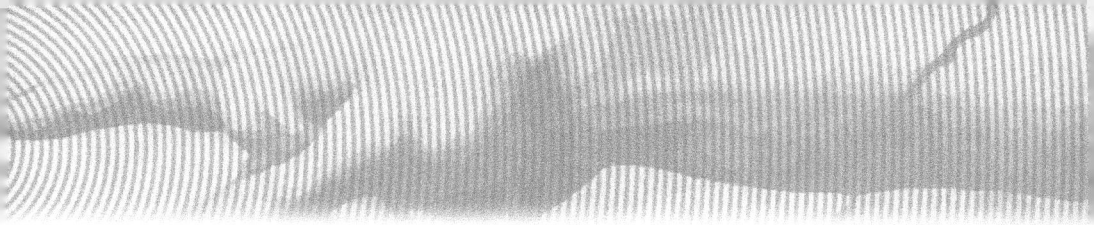

What would happen if the people closest to you were asked to describe your private integrity? Would their answer match your public persona?

_____

_____

_____

_____

_____

_____

Have you ever been tempted to lead from a place of entitlement rather than example? What consequences followed that mindset?

_____

_____

_____

_____

_____

_____

What three truths or insights impacted you most from this book, and what specific steps will you take to live them out?

_____

_____

_____

_____

_____

_____

www.ingramcontent.com/pod-product-compliance
Lightning Source LLC
Chambersburg PA
CBHW070050100426
42734CB00040B/2954